# FOLK ART AND FOLK ARTISTS *in Hungary*

*Károly Gink—Ivor Sándor Kiss*

# FOLK ART
# AND FOLK ARTISTS
*in Hungary*

HASTINGS HOUSE, PUBLISHERS
NEW YORK 10016

TRANSLATED BY ÉVA RÁCZ

TYPOGRAPHY, BINDING AND JACKET BY LAJOS LENGYEL

THE PHOTOGRAPHS WERE TAKEN WITH A PENTACON SIX (VEB PENTACON, DRESDEN)
CAMERA WITH FLEKTOGON AND OLYMPIA SONNAR LENSES (CARL ZEISS, JENA)
CTP AGFA (LEVERKUSEN) COLOUR FILM AND 17, 21, 27, DIN
AGFA (LEVERKUSEN) BLACK-AND-WHITE FILM WERE USED

SECOND EDITION

ISBN 8038—2283—9

LIBRARY OF CONGRESS CATALOG CARD NUMBER 77—165458

© CORVINA, BUDAPEST, 1968
PRINTED IN HUNGARY, 1971
KOSSUTH PRINTING HOUSE, BUDAPEST

# INTRODUCTION

For many centuries Hungarian peasants have fashioned and embellished their objects of everyday use, their work implements, and often their clothes, with great artistry. The Hungarian folk art of today, or more accurately the contemporary applied art of the Hungarian peasantry, is rooted in the rich decorative traditions of the past centuries. It can be clearly established from the material handed down by tradition and from the written records, that this simplified collective art had, in the course of the centuries, several revivals, when it found the strength to create new styles. After each revival it faded only to become reanimated again at each successive renaissance with a much broader social range through the intermediary of classical traditions.

Dealing with the part played by traditions, C. P. Saintyves, one of the great experts in French folklore, wrote in his *Manuel de folklore*, published in 1933: "Folklore is a study of traditions, and for this reason its first task is to collect and classify the facts that make up tradition; after this it must explain their nature or traditional essence... Folk tradition cannot be compared to buried treasure: it is a flow of all kinds of richness, an infinite succession of thousands of human inventions enjoyed by the peoples of civilized nations. Traditions, like the stars, perform the miracle of perpetual motion."

"Let us take good care," wrote Gyula Juhász, one of the most important Hungarian poets of the early twentieth century, "that the people who sing, the people who create myths, the women who draw pictures and the men who carve wood and bone do not become extinct, for their extinction would mean the end of mankind. Let us preserve, collect and disseminate their works; let us learn from them; let their art which is as permanent as nature and as continuous as history become a part of our own living soul."

5

In its wider sense folk art includes poetry, music, customs and dancing; in its more restricted sense it embraces the art of making things, the "instinctive" artistic ability that creates something outstanding in domestic crafts; in other words, peasant decorative art.

Peasant decorative art is a blend of materials, processing techniques, implements and decorative styles that are determined by economic, historical, geographical and climatic factors. These factors exert an influence singly as well as in a combined form.

In Hungary this art has become the specific form of expression of peasant communities. It reflects the taste and desires of the people of remote farmsteads and villages. It is a collective art, for the form, decoration, colours and design of its objects—which have always had a utilitarian purpose—were usually chosen by the community.

The characteristic, basic feature of popular decorative art in every age was the suitability of the material used. This is how a harmony of material, form, decoration, colour and design developed in the objects of folk culture: in the clothes worn for festive and everyday occasions, in bed-covers, linen kerchiefs, objects of use, tools and implements, dwelling houses, farm buildings and in furniture.

Popular taste determined that richness of forms, motifs and patterns in decorative art from which the individual artist drew his inspiration and enabled him to make a more original, useful and attractive object. On the other hand, the experience, insight and expressive ability of the individual artist also contributed to the enrichment of the traditions, techniques and new styles which were being forged. This of course contradicts, and rightly so, the conservative view that "genuine" folk art consists merely of the slavish copying of the motifs and decorative traditions of the past.

The masters of popular decorative art have almost always come from the ranks of the people, from among the peasants or the artisans and small trades-men living in peasant communities. The works of art were generally made for the artist's personal use or as a gift. Nevertheless, the concept of folk art should not be restricted to the activity of craftsmen working for peasant communities. The potters and stove-makers from the fifteenth to eighteenth centuries work-ed in the castles of the aristocracy, in rich mansions and monasteries as well as in the adobe cottages of poor peasants. The potter who was the member of a guild was compelled to move about, or at least attend the fairs and markets, and he probably knew the different tastes of the customers of different regions.

In the course of their journeys, the small tradesmen, the Hungarian furriers, the *szűr* (felt-coat) makers, candle-makers, comb-makers, horn-makers, weavers, dyers and potters incorporated the motifs and decorative elements of several other stylistic centres with the traditional sources of their own community. Though certain elements suggest common origins, the decorative motifs, the compositions—whether patterns or scenes—and the colouring of the work of weavers, spinners and embroidering women are much more varied in their artistic traditions. Their art differs according to the individual geo-graphical regions and ethnic units of Hungary. The forms and decorative expressions of these ethnic units have remained so individual and character-istic that they can still be clearly distinguished. In this way, for instance, the Vásárhely embroidery from the vicinity of Hódmezővásárhely and the Cumanian needlework of the Karcag neighbourhood are today definitely different in composition and colour design, although they are probably of common origin and use the same basic materials, including the decorative wool yarn. On the sodic soil of Cumania the spring flowers of the swampy fields look pale and consequently the floral decoration of the "Cumanian pillow-slips" embroidered in coarse wool looks dimmer. On the other hand, the compositions of Vásárhely folk embroidery feature a larger number of decorative elements, not only the more usual floral motifs, but also sun-flowers, pomegranates, and even stylized birds and butterflies in a much greater variety and splendour of colours.

The differences in the folk art of individual regions appear as variations in form and decorative designs. These differences are especially noticeable in the choice of colours and composition. What remains a common feature, however, in the folk art of all Hungarian landscape units is the pure artistic idiom expressing the cheerfulness or grief of the people and their sincere desire to present the beautiful.

A long historical progress preceded the development of the characteristic styles and techniques of processing material used in Hungarian popular decorative art. The tools and implements employed in their making were also the results of a long historical process. This development can be traced since the fourteenth to sixteenth centuries, from very old objects, such as a few pieces of pottery, a gunpowder container and embroideries. We only have the evidence of written sources on the folk art of earlier times. A few scattered fragments suggest the nomadic way of life, for instance, a salt-cellar made of bark, and beads out of bone.

A greater wealth of relics dating from the Middle Ages is available, in particular glazed and unglazed pottery, stove tiles, blue-and-red and red-and-black coloured homespuns with "cogged" patterns and star motifs, hewn chests, and a few table and chair designs.

Popular decorative art borrowed also from the motifs of the Renaissance, with the forms simplified, of course. Pinks, pomegranates and lilies made their appearance as decorations on textiles and in the arcaded porches of village houses. Nor did the one hundred and fifty years of Turkish occupation pass without leaving their marks. Eastern ornamentation can be discovered in some of the contemporaneous and later pottery as well as in folk embroidery.

The Baroque influence can be seen particularly in the decoration of the wooden gables of houses and in the façades of peasant houses. Carving and all types of woodwork were most typical of this age. The Baroque influence made itself felt in the case of carved furniture and preserved its role as the leading style of peasant cabinet-makers.

The Rococo and particularly the Empire style had much less effect on the forms of peasant furniture, but it encouraged a greater symmetry in the decorative elements.

The embroidery of the *szűr* makers and the furriers, intended mainly for peasants, occasionally featured the Rococo bouquet—in a more concise version but with an obvious stylistic relationship. A later simplification of the Rococo style also appeared on the surface of wooden boxes made with an engraving technique at the end of the nineteenth century.

The *art nouveau*, the dominant stylistic trend at the turn of the century, also left its imprint on folk art, particularly on the pottery of Mohács in South

Hungary and Mezőtúr on the Great Plain. Some elements of *art nouveau* are still exerting an active influence, though in a looser form.

The more prevalent and general folk art styles developed at the end of the eighteenth century and more specifically in the nineteenth century. Depending on the different economic and cultural conditions in the different regions, folk art began to thrive at different times in different places, and it took different courses. Its development culminated in the middle of the nineteenth century, and it began to decline after the turn of the century only, to flourish again in its full splendour after the liberation of Hungary in 1945 when it began to benefit from generous subsidies from the Hungarian state. Folk art, as a great national treasure of Hungarian folk culture, had to be salvaged after World War II; the former peasant art had to be encouraged to find its place under modern social conditions.

In 1953, the Folk Art Council and the National Federation of Domestic Arts and Crafts Cooperatives were founded to provide the proper organization and explore the progressive traditions of folk art. To facilitate the work, the Hungarian state put folk art on a sound financial basis with the Folk Art Fund. The Fund makes millions of forints available annually to promote the development of the new applied folk art. One of the chief uses of the money is in the establishment of regional folk art houses where facilities are provided for folk artists to carry out their creative work.

As a result of these efforts, a unique applied Hungarian folk art developed, catering for every social demand in modern interior decoration. It is attracting an increasing number of admirers and customers to Hungary.

# WEDDING AT BOLDOG

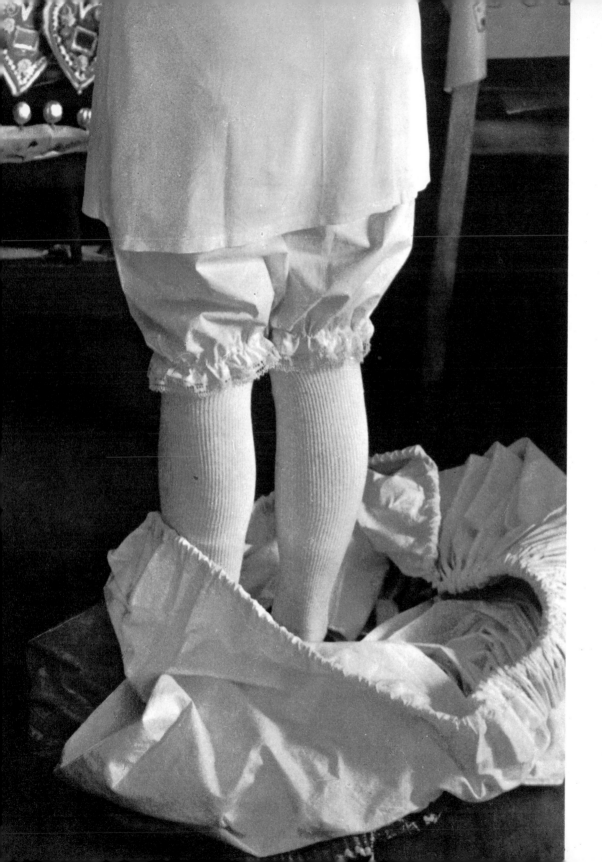

The bride changes

Preparation for the feast

At the wedding
feast

Old honey-cake moulds

# TRANSDANUBIA

Hungary's most varied region is the part of the country that stretches west of the Danube to the Austrian border. The beauty of its wooded hills and rivers and lovely Lake Balaton have undoubtedly contributed to the region's wealth of folk art. The varied profusion of nature offered itself as material and motifs for artistic objects as is evident in the wooden constructions, in the pottery, the herdsmen's creation and in the tools to be found in the region. To trace the origin and development of the colourful folk costumes, the many different kinds of wool and cotton homespuns, the folk embroidery and lace, and the characteristic folk architecture of the region, as well as the local folk customs to which they are related, will still take a great deal of time and labour.

## FOLK POTTERY

Folk pottery is one of the most diversified branches of Transdanubian decorative art. The earthenware dishes of the region vary in form, technique and decoration alike. The basic colour of the Mórágy pottery was white, and was decorated with colourful vegetable motifs, whilst the potters of Püspökbogád ornamented their black dishes with white, green and brown stylized floral designs and lines. In Szekszárd, southern Transdanubia, in the town of János Háry, the fabulous Hungarian hussar, famous for his grandiloquent bragging, earthenware utensils of a reddish terracotta are made with colourful flower motifs. North of the Balaton, Csákvár was the most interesting centre of pottery. The local potters usually shaped their unembellished ware out of fireproof clay, which required a very fine sense of form and subtle craftsmanship. They also made glazed pottery of a pleasant medium-green with engraved ornamentation. The Danubian sailors carried the glazed and unglazed pottery produced at Mohács, a Danube port, to many distant parts. At present, the famous Mohács blackware is popular once more and is being made under the guidance of János Horváth, a potter who has been awarded the title of "Master of Folk Art" for his skill. Mohács blackware comes in a wide range of forms, and their large-size black harvest pitchers and firkins are among the finest pottery forms today.

At Kaposvár, a town to the south of Lake Balaton, the art of folk potters has received a new impetus since the 1950s. Their shops turn out traditional Sárköz-type pottery decorated with a special technique which is of Balkan origin, and consists of coloured lines and stylized elements. This is where, in 1955, the Haban pottery culture, the forms of which were retained in simplified versions in local folk art, was renewed.

The pottery shops of the Tihany Open-Air Museum have been making again, since 1966, the glazed ware typical of the uplands of the Lake Balaton vicinity.

## CARVING

The other important branch of folk art in the hill-country west of the Danube is the herdsmen's skill in carving. The wood of the walnut, pear, plum and cherry trees, of the birch, poplar and willow trees supplied the material for the shepherd carvers, who also used the bones and horns of cattle. The ornamental techniques and the decorations are very varied, and the differences are not simply regional, but result also from the tradition-shaping role of some outstanding artistic personalities who developed new styles.

The techniques of ornamentation known and used in the region are "scratching," "Spanish waxing," "relief carving" and inlay.

In "scratching" the embellishment is scratched into the wood or bone, and then the surface is rubbed with various types of dye. In the next phase, the surface is polished, leaving the coloured decoration only in the scratches, which are shaded darker or lighter according to the depth of the scratch.

Many carvings feature multicoloured decorations. These are usually made with the technique of "Spanish waxing." The place of the motifs is fairly deeply carved out from the surface, and molten wax of the required colour is poured into the hollow and left to harden there. This is how the richly embellished horns, drinking horns, scythe-stone containers, *paprika*-pots and salt-cellars are made. The design of most objects decorated with this technique is concentric with foliation and stylized flowers branching off. The "Spanish wax" technique is also frequently used on carved wooden boxes and mirror frames.

In recent decades, the greatest folk artist in carving was Antal Kapoli, Sr., a shepherd from Somogyhárságy. He not only carved wonderful flutes, but also played them beautifully. He knew all the old songs, ballads and legends of the region. In 1955, he was awarded the Kossuth Prize, the highest state distinction in Hungary.

The most common method of ornamentation is to this day "relief carving." The carver, using this technique, cuts quite deeply into the surface of the material with his sharp knife. With meticulous care he cuts away the unnecessary material, to make his decoration stand out in classic relief. One of the most outstanding masters of this technique is the Transdanubian Ferenc Nagy, whose carved bone work is admirable. With a composition drawn from the ancient Hun and Hungarian myths applied to a large horn, he won the *Grand Prix* for Folk Art at the 1955 World Festival of Youth in Warsaw.

The technique of inlay is really similar to "Spanish waxing," except that the materials used are lead, tin, copper and rubber with the lead and tin inserted in a molten state, and the copper and rubber inlaid in a cold state.

Simple geometrical motifs, human and animal figures, floral and other vegetable designs, and sometimes even entire scenes from the herdsmen's life make up the decorative patterns of carving. The motifs and style of decoration help to determine the age when a given object was made.

The shepherd decorated in particular some of his own implements. He made a richly carved festive crook in addition to his everyday one; the cow-herdsman made a bull-whip; the horse-herdsman—an ornamental long whip decorated with fancy leather plaits and inlay. These implements, by the way, served as symbols for the various kinds of herding. Herdsmen carried these fancy implements of their calling even when they went to market, to a wedding feast or on some official business.

Over two hundred successors of the shepherd carvers are still active folk artists, developing new styles and new ornamental forms. The artistic objects they make have secured a place for themselves in the ethnographical museums of the major European cities.

The art of mask-making is also connected with carving.

## MASQUERADE PROCESSION

Historical Mohács—the town where Hungary lost an important battle against the Turks in 1526—is also noted for a folk custom of obscure, mythical origin, the Masquerade Procession *(busójárás)*. The Southern Slavonic local nationality group, the Sokác, linked the custom with the driving out of the Turks.

Ethnographers, however, generally believe that the procession of masquerades is an ancient carnival custom. On the three days of Shrovetide preceding Lent, there is great merry-making all over the town. The *busós* cover their faces with wooden masks and don short fur cloaks, with the furry side out. They also wear colourful fancy wool stockings and sandals. They hang a bell on their cloak and in their hands they hold rattles and a wooden club with which they make an infernal noise. In this way they march off to frighten the Turks away. The most important rule of the game is gaiety. The route along which the procession marches is lined with men dressed in wedding costumes and veiled women who also take part in the game. These carnival figures are called *maskara*, while the figures wearing the masks are the real *busó*.

To this day two eminent master craftsmen make the *busó* masks. It is a peculiarity of their art that they will never carve two masks of exactly the same design. The carved mask is first painted, then dusted with ash, and then hung up the chimney to get smoked and acquire "old colour." The next step is the decoration of the mask: it is fitted with pierced sheep or cattle horn and lined with sheepskin.

Since relatively few masks are made, they have a rarity value, and after the Masquerade Procession collectors pay high prices for them.

## HOMESPUNS

Homespuns with special designs were usually made by professional weavers, but ordinary peasant women also liked to show off their skill in weaving.

Up to the middle of the nineteenth century, the women made simpler homespuns: pure white for their clothing, and just a few red stripes in their bed-linen, table-cloths and towels. Toward the second half of the nineteenth century, fancy weaving became increasingly popular. These ornamental homespuns were made for festive occasions: to grace the dowry of marriageable girls, their bed-covers and shifts.

In each district the more varied and more colourful homespun patterns reflected the economic position of the local people, but there is evidence also of variation according to the natural features of the region, which is expressed in the application of the designs, their rhythm and in the selection of colours.

The most beautiful homespuns are still made in Western Hungary: in the Sárköz district by the Danube, in the nearby Sokác villages of Alsószentmárton and Felsőszentmárton, and in Csányoszró, a typical village in the interesting Ormánság district.*

There are four villages—Öcsény, Decs, Sárpilis and Báta—which belong to the Sárköz district in the narrowest sense, but usually Sióagárd, Szeremle and Váralja are also included in the landscape unit. After the river regulations in the middle of the nineteenth century, the soil of Sárköz became fertile. This helped its folk art to attain peerless splendour. Its homespuns have their entire surface covered with rich decorative patterns. Black and red, white and red, and black and white are their traditional colour schemes. More recently they have interwoven bronze-brown, green, light blue and also silver and gold threads.

In the County of Baranya, the Hungarian, Sokác, Croatian and German ethnical groups have preserved their traditional folk costumes in many areas.

---

* Ormánság: A province of 45 villages in Southern Hungary, a marshy area at the junction of several rivers. Due to its situation, it has developed over the centuries as an ethnic group with its own characteristic style of costume, construction and dialect.

Their homespuns are of many types, with an extraordinary wealth of colours and richness of design.

This same riot of colours and motifs appears in the wool homespuns of the villages by the Dráva river. These ornamental designs originally graced the festive aprons of the women, but they can also be found on the prayer-rugs which the women used to take along to church and put under their knees. In the Ormánság, the homespuns are made in blue or red geometrical designs against a white background.

## FOLK EMBROIDERY

Among the Hungarian folk embroideries those of Transdanubia hold a distinguished place.

Especially beautiful are the white embroidery motifs of the sling-shaped headdress of the Sárköz district and the motifs of the border of the shawl in fiery red. This ornamental mode is of Byzantine origin and made its way to Hungary via the Turks.

The embroidery motifs of the women's folkwear of Sióagárd, a village in Sárköz, have been transposed to table-cloths and runners suitable for modern use as wall decoration.

Buzsák is a village close to the southern coast of Lake Balaton. Buzsák embroidery is one of the most popular types of needlework in Hungary. Its main ornamental motifs are roses linked together with straight lines and stylized leaves. The basic colours are red and blue. Another well-known folk embroidery style is that of Karád. Here the linen is decorated by open-work arranged in various patterns and the eyelets embroidered in coloured yarn.

27

A wide-spread, popular white embroidery is to be found in the neighbourhood of the North-Transdanubian communities of Hövej and Kapuvár, where scarfs and shawls to be worn on the head and shoulders were embellished with eyelet embroidery and satin-stitching. The basic material is the finest cambric and the embroidery demands a highly skilled stitching technique.

Transdanubian landscape, with the Szt. György-hegy

(St. George Hill) in the background

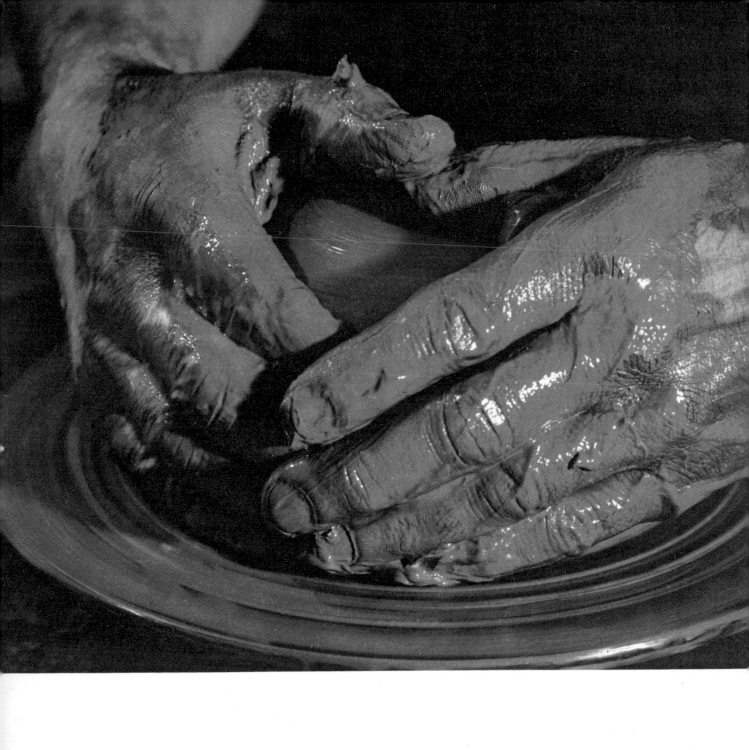

Jug being turned
on the potter's wheel
at Mohács

The jugs are being fired

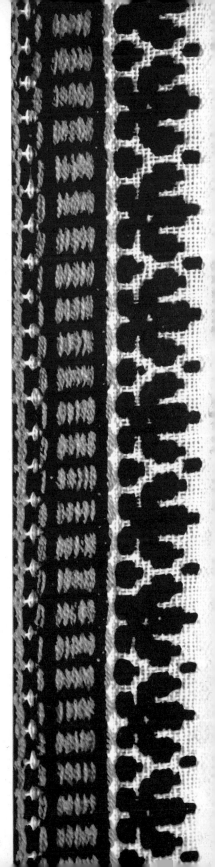

Pattern-weaving

women and a pattern

Detail of a Sárköz peasant bed

Sokác woollen homespuns

Sokác women in their folk-wear

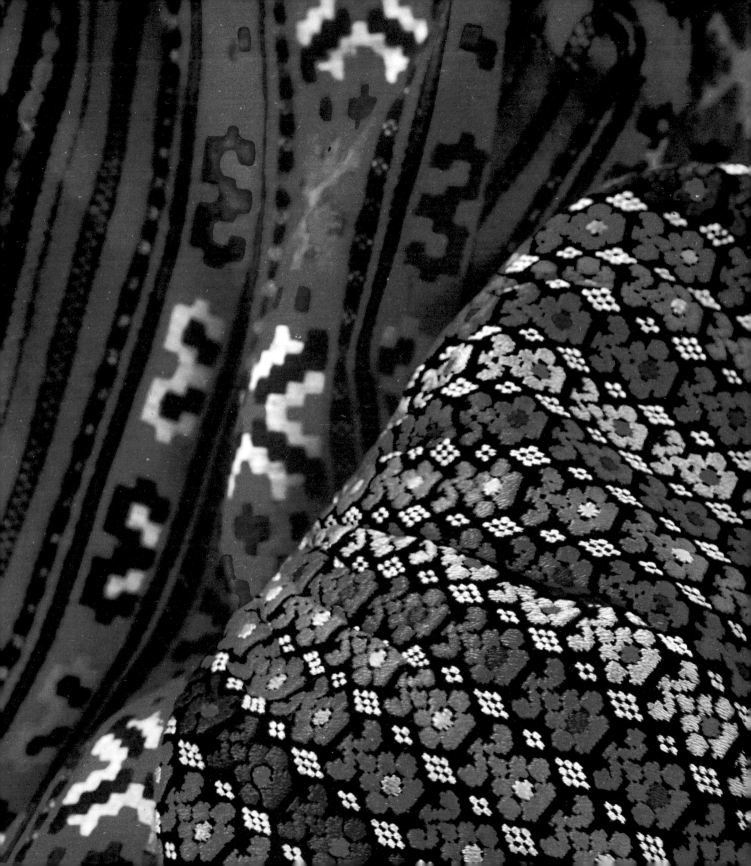

Sokác woman
at the bobbin

Sokác women

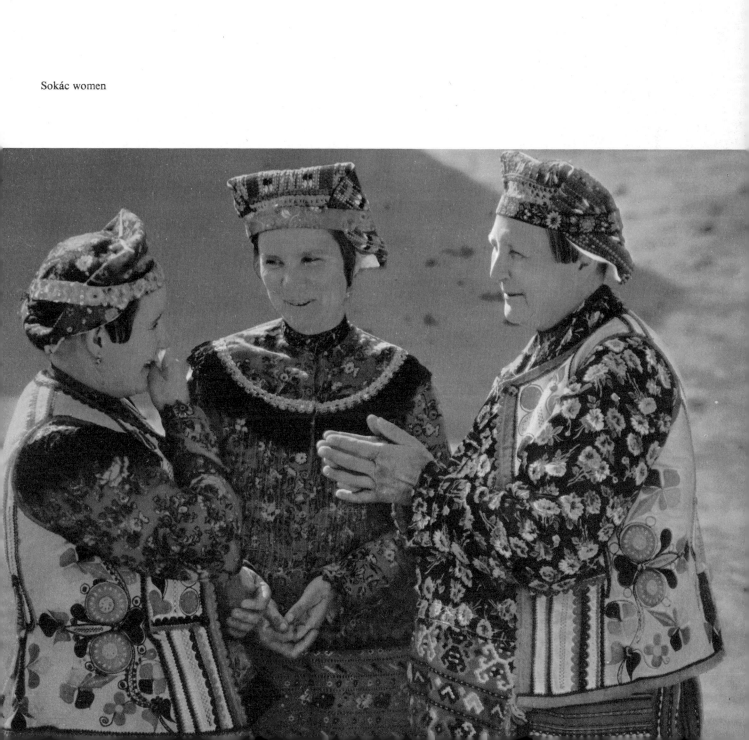

A Mohács

peasant

Detail
of a kitchen
with an open
fireplace

◁ Embroidery
from Buzsák
with star design

Embroidering
women
at Buzsák

Sióagárd wear

"Writing" the pattern on a plate in the Sárköz district

Peasant figure in clay from Sárköz

Painted shel

The prow of the water-mill of Ráckeve

◁ Relief carving

Wood-carved peasant
figure wearing the *suba*

Relief carving

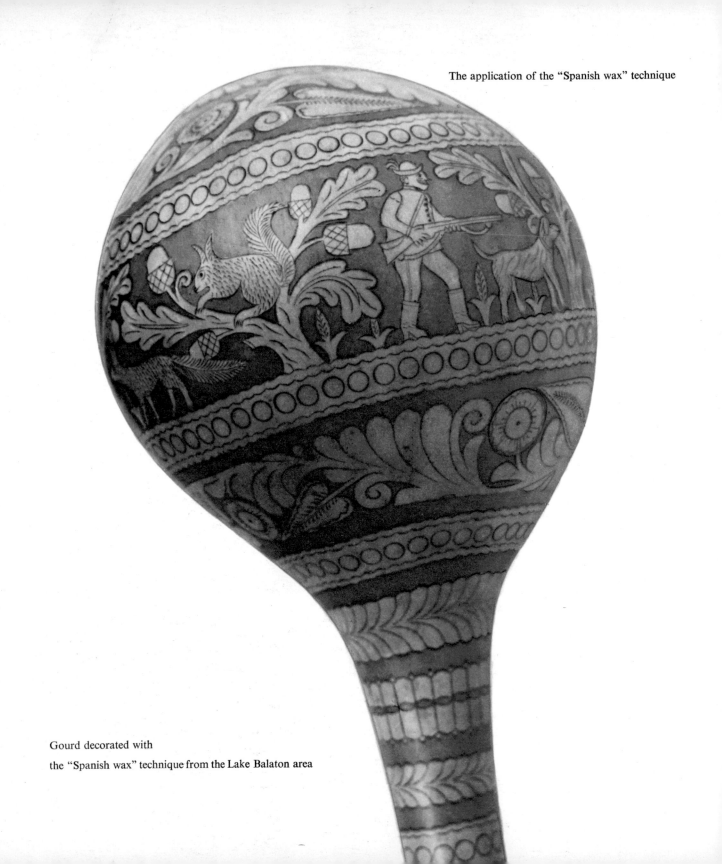

Gourd decorated with

the "Spanish wax" technique from the Lake Balaton area

Painted peasant chests

Carved gunpowder flask

Wooden graveposts

Fishermen's gear from the Sárköz
district by the Danube

The catch

Basket weaving

Hövej embroidery

Grape treading ▷

(bone carving)

Wooden flasks decorated with leather

# THE HIGHLANDS OF NORTHERN HUNGARY

In the northern highlands of Hungary, to the north and south of the Ipoly river, lives an ethnical group called the Palóc. Partly owing to the economic conditions and partly, perhaps, to the closed-in character of the highland district consisting of the Börzsöny, Mátra and Bükk Mountains, the folk art of the area has preserved many of its old features. In some of the peasant houses the visitor can still see the hewn chest resembling the ancient sarcophagus, and the benches and chairs with open-work carved back-rests made by peasants. Their ornamentation is usually figurative mixed with vegetable elements.

Among the carvings of the herdsmen of the region the typical wooden drinking cup, the *csanak* (chanak) is the best known. The handle is usually shaped in the form of human or animal figures.

## FOLK-WEAR AND EMBROIDERY

Among the highland folk costumes the most famous are those of the Palóc, especially in the villages of Őrhalom, Rimóc, and Hollókő, but also the similar folkwear in Boldog and Tura, and by the River Galga, belong to this group. The folk-wear of the area shows simple moderation as well as exaggerated splendour. Sándor Petőfi, the great nineteenth-century Hungarian poet, wrote in a letter about his visit to this district:

"... My journey led through the village of Ludány, where I saw the most beautiful coifs in my life. If I get married, I shall have coifs brought from there for my wife."

Of all the Palóc folk customs, the wedding feast attended by a colourful crowd and featuring clever rhymed sayings, was the most interesting.

The embroidery of the Palóc region is no less characteristic than that of Transdanubia; the closed, isolated character of the highlands influenced their development.

The embellishments of the Tura folkwear were the shift, shawl, and head-scarf, each of noble simplicity and decorated with meticulous white embroidery. In recent years, the designs have become moderately colourful. The principal motifs are asters, hearts, doves and other birds. The colouring is blue and red, and there is a rhythmic alternation of dark and light blues.

Formerly the counterpanes and the sheet borders were embroidered in the Palóc district. This embroidery has preserved a very old pinking technique. The local folk embroidery has been revived at Recsk in the Mátra district. Geometric designs constitute the principal motifs.

Mezőkövesd is the principal settlement of the Matyó ethnical group. The popular Vachot's Calendar, published in 1860, wrote of them: "...They took their name from King Matthias*, who gave them more liberty, and in fact issued and signed a writ for them at Mezőkövesd, whereupon they were called the sons of Matthias and later Matyós." The folkwear and folk embroidery of the Matyó villages are unique. The Matyós were landless people who hired themselves out to perform agricultural work in other districts of the country, but despite their poverty developed a splendidly colourful and varied decorative style that can be followed since the 1880s. The oldest Matyó embroidery is simple linen embroidery on sheet borders in red and blue. Their earliest type of work is the furriers' embroidery with which they decorated the *kuzsu*, a waist-length jacket with fur lining. Although the furriers' embroidery was

78

* Matthias Corvinus (1458–1490) the famous Renaissance ruler of Hungary.

the product of a male craft, the motifs and the colours affected the women's needlework. According to the legend that purports to explain the symbolism of the colours used in Matyó decorative work, black represents the soil from which life sprang, red is the colour of summer, light and joy, while blue stands for grief and death.

Matyó folk embroidery has become popular throughout the world.

## HOMESPUNS

The weaving women of the region have preserved the simple designs of the old Palóc homespuns. The patterns of the decorative stripes are hard; the colour schemes are white, red and blue, or white, red and black.

In the last two decades one of the valuable Hungarian folk art traditions was revived in the village of Heves and its vicinity, which is part of the Palóc district. For long decades there had been no weaving in this district and even the simpler designs were forgotten.

Since 1953, there is a trend to revive and rediscover local traditions and women were taught to weave again. The simple ornamental technique of the traditional Palóc homespun was improved with the cross-stitches in a more diffcult technique. The principal motifs are birds, doves, chicks, dolls, stars and flowers, in red, old-gold and blue, red-and-blue and green against a white background.

## WROUGHT-IRON WORK

A few years ago the making of wrought-iron work received a new impetus in the village of Átány.

Pál Ivák, a peasant smith, collected the iron crests of old peasant houses. In his shop he shapes the still glowing material of rustic candle-sticks, wall-vases and lamp-posts into "stork," "Hussar's moustachio," and "round-bar flowers." The iron fittings made on the model of old treasure chests also recall traditional decorative elements.

Village in the Bükk Mountains

Embroidery

from Recsk

Gable of a peasant
house at Átány

◁ A Palóc house with open attic

Detail of a room with homespun pillows

Painted Palóc cradle

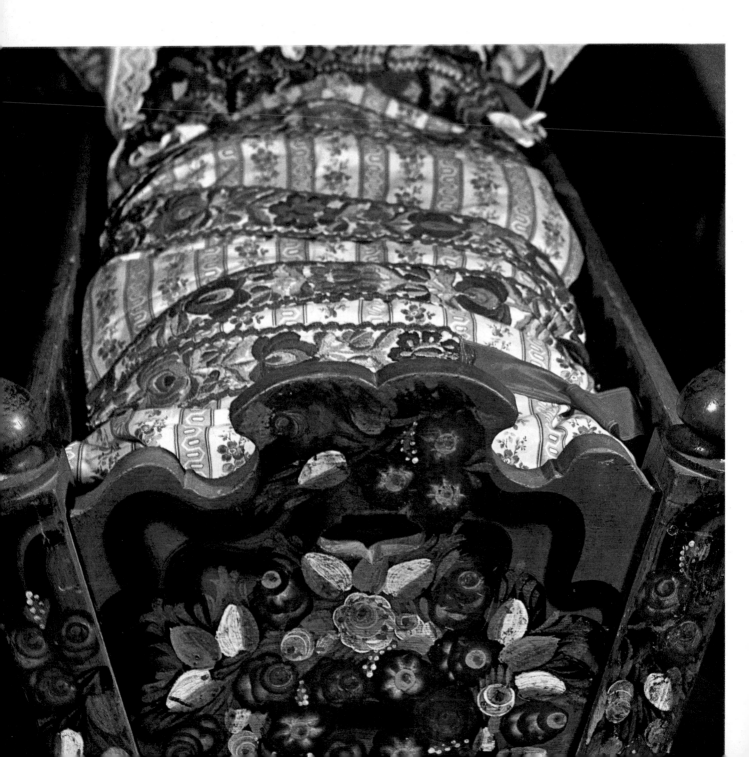

Palóc furniture

Pál Ivák, iron-smith of Átány and his works

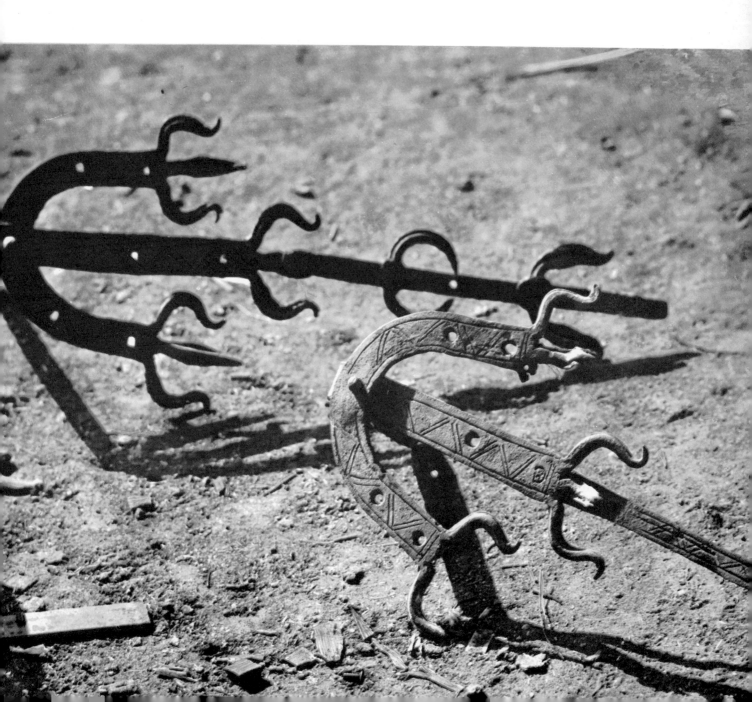

◁ Boldog costumes

Young wife of Hollókő

This is the way
to make
a Palóc coif

Old Matyó
women

◁ Interior of a Matyó
peasant house

The late
Bori Kisjankó,
Matyó designer

Matyó embroidery

Matyó women,
embroidering

Details from the
Bori Kisjankó
Memorial
Museum
of Mezőkövesd

# THE GREAT HUNGARIAN PLAIN

The lowlands of the Great Hungarian Plain not only inspired poets to write beautiful verse, but, with its distant horizons and abundant sunlight, it also encouraged the development of characteristic folk art.

It is an interesting ethnographical fact about the Great Plain that here the towns played an important part in the development of folk art. The cities of Debrecen, Kecskemét and Szeged, with their well-attended markets and large artisan population, determined the general taste in their vicinities. An outstanding example is the town of Hódmezővásárhely, in the south-eastern part of Hungary, where at the end of the nineteenth century more than four hundred potters worked in three different parts of the town, each of the three groups making different forms and decorating them in different ways.

There is a remarkable dual characteristic of the state of the decorative art in the Great Plain. After the 1840s hardly any painted furniture was made here, and only very few embroidered pillow-slips and sheets have been handed down to posterity. In the same place, however, the art of pottery continued to flourish in the second half of the last century and at the turn of the century.

## POTTERY

Because of its central location, the Great Hungarian Plain formed a link in the development of the different pottery cultures in Transdanubia, Northern Hungary and Transylvania. Nevertheless, highly individual pottery was made in the lowland shops.

At Hódmezővásárhely, plates and bowls were made at every shop in a wide variety of forms. For this reason the potters were called here "bowl-makers." This traditional pursuit is carried on today by Sándor Vékony, a potter of

Hódmezővásárhely, whose glazed pottery is, on account of the fine work and pure colours, among the most valuable products of the craft. He likes to use white for his basic colour with blue lined, so-called "written" decoration.

The jug-makers of Mezőtúr usually made earthenware dishes. Today the pottery of the Great Plain flourishes most at this place where there are altogether over eighty local potters.

One of the most important junctions of the mid-Tisza pottery culture was Tiszafüred. Today only a single master, Sándor Kántor of Karcag, carries on the pottery traditions of Tiszafüred.

The making of unglazed blackware can look back on several centuries of history in the Great Plain, but by the beginning of this century the craft had sunk into oblivion. Since the 1950s, Lajos Fazekas, Sr. and his sons at Nád-udvar, close to Debrecen, resumed the production of finely shaped black jugs, jars and oil-lamps.

At Karcag, István Rusói, a "Master of Folk Art," revived the art of stove tiles in 1955. He retained the traditional forms, but expanded the colour range, and improved on the technique of tile decoration by scratching in animal figures and vegetable designs. István Rusói's tile mouldings with bird designs are highly decorative.

## CARVING AND FOLK-WEAR

Old ways of animal husbandry survived for a long time on the vast pasture lands of the Great Plain, and consequently the herdsmen's art attained a high standard in this region, particularly if one considers the decoration of horn objects, leather plaiting and the folk-wear of the region.

The *szűr* or felt-coat is one of the most ancient pieces of clothing in general use in Hungary. It was exclusively worn by men, and always thrown over the shoulders. Since men rarely put their arms in them, the sleeves lost their original significance. The fancy *szűr* was the Hungarian peasant's festive dress practically all his life-time.

*Szűr*s were the handiwork of *szűr*-tailors, which was a distinct trade. The material was usually white frieze on which the embroidery was stitched in red and black, or, more rarely, yellow and blue yarn. *Szűr*-tailors called this work "flowering." The motifs consisted of stylized roses, tulips, carnations and lilies-of-the-valley, all motifs which have survived in present-day folk art.

Another method of embellishing the *szűr* is by the appliqué technique. The motifs were borrowed from embroidery, and hence roses and carnations and other flowers ornament the surface. Cherries and tobacco leaves are a typical *szűr* design.

The water flask constituted an essential piece of equipment for the herdsman. This was made of wood, but coated with colt hide, which helped to insulate it. The colt-hide-decorated flask is today an ornamental object, but one which is marked by the beauty of Great Plain craftsmanship.

## EMBROIDERY

At Hódmezővásárhely and in Great Cumania, in the vicinity of the town of Karcag, an interesting type of embroidery has survived: the "hairy" embroidery. It calls for the use of hairy crewel made from the wool of the long-fleeced Hungarian sheep on coarse linen. The floral motifs are subtly shaded, one shade blending into the next with gentle transitions.

Similar to the freely drawn "hairy" embroidery is the Orosháza cross-stitch done in crewel with a special technique. By the end of the last century, the technique had sunk into oblivion and was revived only in 1964.

Kalocsa needlework is among the most popular folk embroidery, especially since the Kalocsa folk-wear has survived to this day. On the costumes of the unmarried girls wearing blue ribbons and the young women wearing coifs, the stylized flowers look resplendent in twenty-seven hues. "Writing women" draw the design on white or pastel-coloured fabrics. The patterns are usually a stylized or natural flower composition. Daisies, marigolds, cornflowers, poppies, lilies, tulips, roses and lilies-of-the-valley furnish the floral motifs.

*

Coloured wall painting, a kind of decorative folk art almost unparalleled in Europe, is in vogue at Kalocsa. Without even first outlining the design, the so-called "painting women" paint on the white-washed walls colourful stylized flower compositions which fill in the entire surface. To adopt the genre for contemporary interior decoration, Kalocsa designs are now applied to wall-paper.

The Bridge of Nine Holes at Hortobágy

Pegs for jugs hung
with folk pottery

Tiszafüred pottery

Peasant figures ▷
by Sándor Kántor
(Grand Prix,
1959, Brussels)

Old flask
from Tiszafüred

Fancy *szűr*
from the Great
Hungarian Plain

Sheep in Bugac                                    Hungarian shepherd puli

Bobbin
lace from
the Great
Hungarian
Plain

Peasant
homespun
with fringe
trimming

Cumanian embroidered pillow-slips

Interior of Cumanian House of Folk Art ▷

Nádudvar jug

Nádudvar pottery—before firing

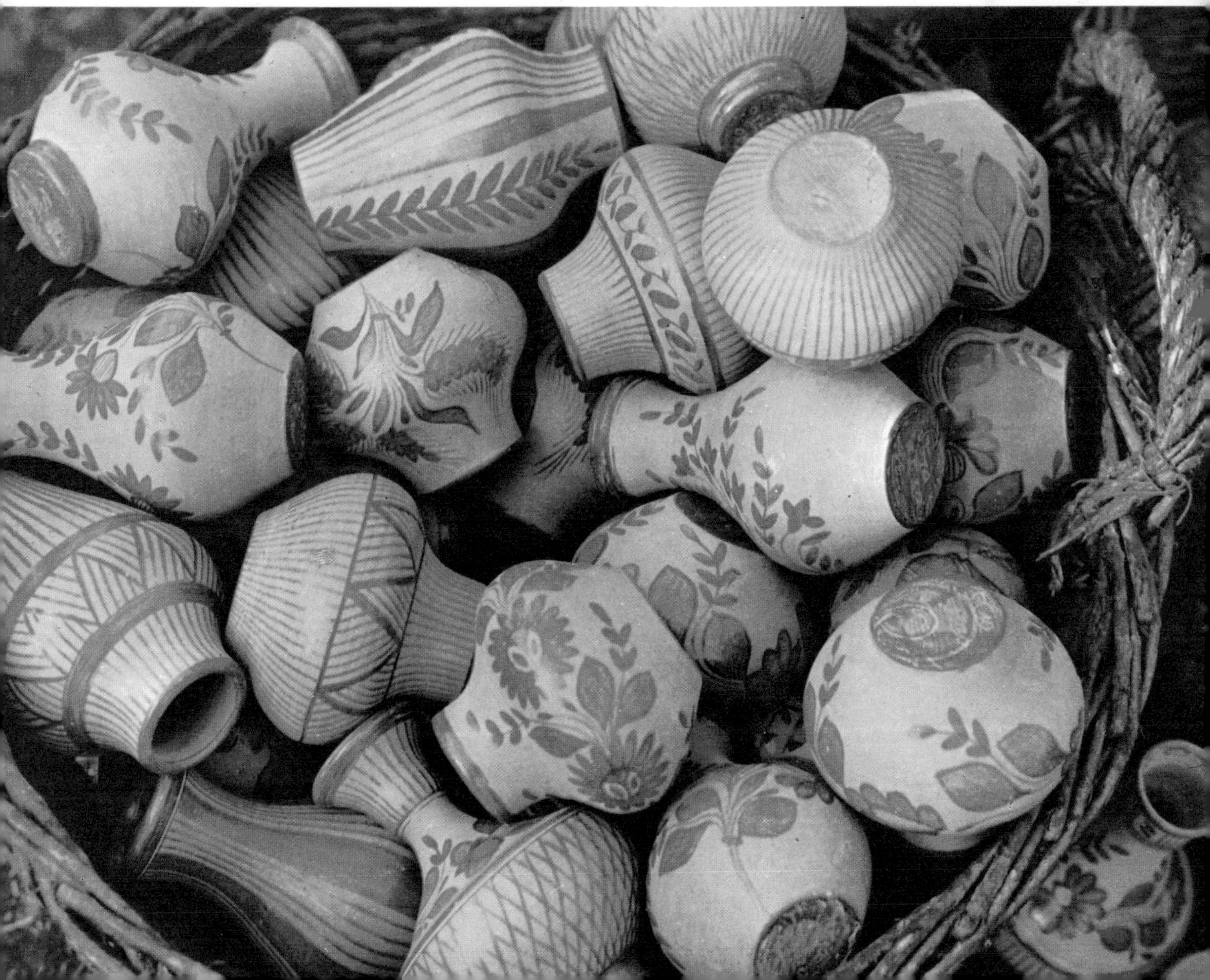

Interior of kitchen at the Kalocsa House of Folk Art

Wall-painting at Kalocsa

Cowherd's reed hut

in the Hortobágy

Wall of cowherd's
hut with bells

Hortobágy horse-herds

Five-in-hand

The *puszta* in winter

*Busó* Masquerade Procession at Mohács

A *busó* mask